GRIMORIUM

IMPERIUM

THE BOOK OF THE OLD SPIRITS

JOHN DEE

by Victor Shaw

Erebus Society

Erebus Society

First published in Great Britain in 2018
by Erebus Society

First Edition

Copyright of Text © Victor Shaw 2018
Cover & illustration copyright © Constantin Vaughn 2018

ISBN: 978-1-912461-13-4

www.erebussociety.com

Grimoirium Imperium
or
The Book of the Old Spirits

Is the Book of the Law and Practices of the Sleeping
Dead by Doctor John Dee.

The Conjuration of All Manner of Chaotic Spirits
Secret Seals and Talismans
The Truth of the Old Spirits
and
The Ultimate Keys to Life and Death and the Universe

Table of Contents

Introduction...I

Liber Primum 1
Liber Secundum.. 17
Liber Tertium 41
Liber Quartum.. 61

Introduction
by Dr. John Dee

This is the book of powerful conjurations and subjugations of demons and Gods which dwell in far away places, places which are past north and south, east and west, up and down, places which are even beyond the Earth and the farthest planets, places which are far from the creation of God. The secrets which I shall tell of were not learned until late in my life, when in 1601 I started to translate a manuscript which I had owned for many years, but had not cared much for. I cared not for it because it was given to me by the fraudulent Barnabas Saul as a present to me so that we should part as friends, despite the lies and deceptions he had told to me. I received the manuscript from Saul in 1581 and I kept it in my library for many years and would have given it to anyone who asked for it, that was how little I cared for it - oh, how glad I am that I did not part with it, for now I realise how important the text is! In the late days of 1601 I felt curious about the book and wondered if it was as valuable as Saul had told me before we parted company. The manuscript said that it was the word of Abd Al-Hazred, who had learned much of the secret art of conjuration from avatars and spirits that he met whilst travelling in the desert. When I first practised the rituals which were described in this book, it was then that I realised it's importance, for here was the most powerful book ever to be written by mortal hand.

But I bid thee to beware! For the book gripped me with a desire to devote myself completely to it, and I found that I had developed a mania for it. Much of my other writing stopped and all matters of humanity became unimportant to me. This desire for the book made me devote many of my waking hours to it, and I experienced many horrific things, but I also found out many most secret secrets. I wish that I had more time on this mortal plane to study the book, for even now I see that it contains the key to many unfathomable mysteries, including the mysteries of life and death and even the secrets of the Creator himself. Please listen to this final warning before you read further;

The book attracts many demons to it, even now they will be watching you, invisible. I urge that you pray that they are gone and banish each time you turn a page, otherwise you may find yourself overcome by them, which would doubtlessly mean madness and death.

Liber Primum

This is the book of the laws and practices of the sleeping dead, written by myself, Abd Al-Hazred - the great sorcerer and poet. With the secrets in this book I have spoken with dark spirits, who have furnished me with many riches, both in the form of money and knowledge, I have even learned the unlearnable knowledge of the divine ones, such is the power of what I learned. I have also learned of the Old Spirits, who lived before man, and still live dreaming, and they are very terrible. It was a face of one of these very spirits that initiated me into this powerful magic.

One morning I awoke to see that the world had changed, the sky was darker and rumbled with the voices of evil spirits and flowers and life had been strangled by them also. Then I heard the screaming call, the screaming of something beyond the hills which was calling me. The screaming call maddened me and made me sweat, in the end I could not ignore it and decided to find what manner of beast was making the screaming call. I left my house and set out into the desert with the call sounding all around me. In the desert I wandered, without anything but the clothes that I was wearing, I sweated during the day and froze during the night. But still the screaming call kept on.

On the third day, on the eighteenth hour of that day, the screaming call stopped and standing in front of me was a man. The man was completely black, both in face and clothing, and he greeted me in my tongue and with my name. The man told me his name and his name was Ebonor and he was a demon. Ebonor was the one who had made the screaming call and I did not yet know that he was more than the lesser demon that torments the infirm, he was the messenger of the most evil spirits called the Old Spirits, which even the most powerful sorcerer of even God cannot completely control. This demon gave me the gift to understand all languages, whether it be written or spoken or of man or beast. This is why I, Abd Al-Hazred, have been able to read documents which have confused many lesser mortals for many decades, but I have also been able never to get peace. For even when I try to lay down and sleep, I can hear the creatures around me speaking, I can hear the birds and the desert insects, but worst of all the dogs, which madly growl and bark about the coming of the Old Spirits.

Now that the screaming call had ceased, I returned to my town with my new knowledge and had many sleepless nights, listening to the sound of the smallest beast and invisible demons talking, only where everything is dead could I ever sleep, thought I.

After many days without sleep I set out into the desert once more, hoping to find Ebonor and to make him take back his gift, for I had found it to be a most terrible curse. For three days and eighteen hours I wandered again and on the eighteenth hour Ebonor appeared to me. I fell before him and begged him to take back his gift as it was driving my mind away from me, but he did not show any compassion. Instead he said that he would show me more knowledge. He took my hand and led me beneath the cold desert sands, down many sets of steps, untrod by man, until we reached the door to a secret chamber. In here, you shall find the ultimate truths, but you shall only understand a little, said the demon to me as he opened the door. Then I heard the screaming call coming from the portal, but this time it was a thousand times more intense and Ebonor took my hand and pulled me across the threshold. Through that door I saw all the untold knowledge, although only a little has my mind retained.

And when the learning was at an end, I found myself back in the desert standing by Ebonor, who laughed at me and jested that the mind of man was much inferior to that of the Old Spirits. I had learned of the Old Spirits in the secret chamber, they were most terrible and evil spirits who came from outside creation to live upon the earth. Then at a time before man was born they were expelled from the earth because the stars became wrong. All were expelled from the earth except for Nyarlathotep, the dark one or Egypt and the messenger of the Old Spirits, of which Ebonor was one face. Turning away from me, Ebonor laughed again and said to me that one day a time will come when the stars are right again and the Old Spirits shall return. With this having been said, I was alone once more.

I decided to rest, although my cursed gift was still with me. It was when I rested that I realised that I was holding a book, the book contained the many names of Nyarlathotep, the Old Spirit's messenger. I was able to read this book perfectly, but no one else was able to, for they said that they could not understand the words on the pages. The book told me that Nyarlathotep has twenty-one names, or faces. Each of these names may be called upon in their correct hours, from the third hour in the day to the penultimate hour in the day. With each name is a sacred and special sign, which must also be used with the correct invocation. The names of Nyarlathotep are thus;

The name of the third hour is Etonetatae and he is master of magical words and phrases and he should be consulted much in your work, for he will deliver to you many words of power. Etonetatae has no body, but may manifest as a mist or may remain invisible.

Note: All of Nyarlathotep's seals except for the final one are made from three lines and three curves.

The name of the fourth hour is Odanen, who brings with him the wishes of the Old Spirits, you may wish to communicate with Odanen, rather than with the Old Spirits themselves, for it is many times safer. Odanen will appear before the magician as a shadowy figure who is only just visible.

The name of the fifth hour is Banibo, who will reveal to the magician the whereabouts of splendid treasures, but be warned - do not let him persuade you to leave your circle, be sure to get the directions from him and then banish him. Banibo appears as a deformed and bloated man and emanated the odour of rotting matter.

The name of the sixth hour is Obinab, who will reveal to the magician many secrets concerning the universe. He is Banibo's opposite, but he will still urge you to leave the circle so that he may take you on a journey. If he does this then insist that he himself gives you the knowledge which would be attained from the journey.

The name of the seventh hour is Bosoro, who will appear as a huge and fiery snake - do not look into it's eyes or you shaall be trapped forever, but command him to appear in human form and he will have to obey. Bosoro has the knowledge of men's minds and you may ask him to reveal the knowledge of a man which you shall name.

The name of the eighth hour is Oxeren, who has knowledge of the future and will appear on a black horse, which can run faster than time itself.

The name of the ninth hour is Badero, who is the lord of gestures and will teach the conjurer many magical gestures, with which he shall be able to open gates to other places or effect the minds of men.

The name of the tenth hour is Osenin, who has control over the bodies of men and can change a man into any shape the magician tells him. Osenin appears with the body of a man and the head of a lizard, which is enveloped in flame.

The name of the eleventh hour is Boxebo, who will make doors open for the magician so that his way is not restricted. Boxebo appears as a huge insect with many pairs of hands.

The name of the twelfth hour is Norano, who knows of all the books which have ever existed and she will dictate to the magician whichever book he seeks at that time. Norano appears as a winged scribe.

The name of the thirteenth hour is Onaron, who has much knowledge of the sciences which he will tell to the magician and he may even be commanded to bring to the magician rare materials, such as herbs and stones. Onaron appears a winged man with many long and sharp teeth.

The name of the fourteenth hour is Nerexo, who holds information about secret talismen and seals. Nerexo appears in the form of an old man with the legs of a goat.

The name of the fifteenth hour is Reranber, who is a most evil spirit and will murder any man at your command. Reranber will appear as a prince in shimmering gold holding a black sword.

The name of the sixteenth hour is Orosob, who is a most lustful demon and will procure any woman that the magician wishes. Orosob appears as an unclothed black man and if he does not appear it is because he is walking the land ravishing the unwary, so you should call him again, but do not call him more than three times or you shall enrage him.

The name of the seventeenth hour is Nineso, who will appear exactly like the magician. Nineso has the power to conjure many lesser spirits and the magician should command him which spirits he should conjure.

The name of the eighteenth hour is Ebonor, who will reveal the knowledge that is not of man and also understands all languages. The magician should question him and should not urge him to give the gifts of knowledge and language, as he gave to me - for to do so would anger him. Ebonor will appear as a black man, clothed in a black robe.

The name of the nineteenth hour is Oredab, who appears as a skeleton riding atop a great lizard. Oredab has the power to destroy whole cities in one gesture.

The name of the twentieth hour is Nenado who has much strength and can effect the movement of the stars and planets. Nenando will appear with the body of a statue and the head of a fly larvae.

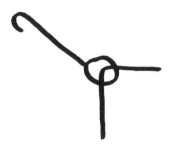

The name of the twenty-first hour is Rubanir, who's appearance changes constantly and will always be unidentifiable. Rubanir has knowledge of all things past.

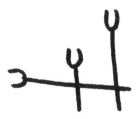

The name of the twenty-second hour is Obexob, who appears as the floating corpse of a pharaoh enveloped in flames. Obexob will deliver visions to the magician who studies the flames closely.

The name of the twenty-third hour is Etananesoe, who is too terrible to behold. Etananesoe is the true incarnation of Nyarlathotep and will only appear at the time when the stars are right for himself.

Those are the twenty-one names of Nyarlathotep and the name may be summoned at the appropriate hour using the conjurations which I shall set down later in my writing, be warned though - do not summon more than one face in a day, otherwise Nyarlathotep will become enraged and break the circle, devouring the magician.

With the book containing this knowledge, I set about seeking a new abode, for I could not return to my village, for I needed time to study the ways of the Old Spirits and I needed a dead place, so that I could sleep undisturbed. After many days of walking I eventually found myself at the cavernous ruins of a city, which was once called Ubar, this was where I decided to dwell. In my solitude I was able to practice my art and learned much from the names of Nyar-lathotep and I even dared to conjure some of the Old Spirits, with very grave consequences, for I was not prepared for the destruction they would cause - for no circle can hold them. I also wwrote down all that I learned that was writeable so that this knowledge may be passed on and shall not be lost again.

Liber Secundum

In this chapter I shall reveal the names, natures and seals of the Old Spirits. Once the Old Spirits lived on the earth, but when the stars changed they were expelled and separated. There are, however, times when the stars become right for certain spirits and these are the times which they can be summoned on. There are forty-five Old Spirits who are very terrible and very powerful, for this reason I ask you never to summon them apart from in exceptional situations. If you do risk summoning then almost certain death shall await if you have not made the appropriate preparations - for they cannot be banished easily and will inflict terrible damage once summoned. The stars become right for the Old Spirits as the zodiac's band travels across the heavens and the times upon which they may be conjured upon shall now be revealed.

Starting seven degrees from the Archer's sign and proceeding deosil, I shall work my way around the wheel of the zodiac, explaining when the stars are right for each of the Old Spirits.

𝔍n the seventh to the thirteenth degrees the stars are right for Uk-Han, who appears as a huge, horned snake.

Note: Each seal also has an appropriate zodiacal sign by it's side. These signs date from circa 2bc.

𝔍n the fourteenth to twentieth degrees the stars are right for Magoth, who appears like a large and strange cat creature with the tentacles of a squid on it's front.

In the twenty-first to twenty-seventh degrees the stars are right for Yak-Ishath, which appears as something too terrible to behold - an ever changing mass featuring the faces of the souls it has swallowed.

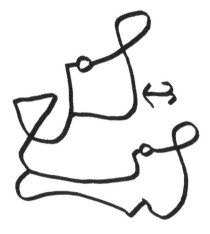

In the twenty-eighth to thirty-fourth degrees the stars are right for Lunigguroth, who appears as a sphere of glowing white, from which vast multitudes of horrors pour.

In the thirty-fifth to forty-first degrees the stars are right for Tursoth, who appears as a giant scale covered man with the legs of a spider.

In the forty-second to forty-eight degrees the stars are right for Marbel, who has no body, but the sound will be most apparent, causing ears to bleed and animals to fall down dead.

In the forty-ninth to fifty-fifth degrees the stars are right for Diabaka, who appears as a huge, flaming monstrosity, surrounded by fiery suns.

In the fifty-sixth to sixty-second degrees, nothing may be summoned, not even the lesser faces of Nyarlathotep, for this is a time when the stars are wrong for every denomination of Old Spirit.

In the sixty-third to sixty-ninth degrees the stars are right for Cthuhanai, who appears as a great winged man with the head of a decaying lizard bird.

In the seventieth to seventy-sixth degrees the stars are right for Nagoango, who shall appear from the ground and try to swallow you whole.

In the seventy-seventh to eighty-third degrees the stars are right for Vagonch, who will appear as a huge mass of whiteness which will swallow anything which comes near.

In the eighty-fourth to ninetieth degrees the stars are right for Pul-Marg, who shall appear as a black demon with the power to petrify the people who's gaze he catches.

In the ninety-first to ninety-seventh degrees the stars are right for Bovadoit, who cannot be summoned because of her size and terribleness. Bovadoit shall be locked out until the stars are fully right.

In the ninety-eight to one-hundred and fourth degrees the stars are right for Parahan, who shall appear as a great dragon, but with a small, many eyed head.

During the one-hundred and fifth to the one-hundred and eleventh degrees, nothing may be conjured.

In the one-hundred and twelfth to one-hundred and eighteenth degrees the stars are right for Yurnal, which shall appear as a great gray and lumbering thing, too vast for the eye to view.

During the one-hundred and nineteenth to the one-hundred and twenty-fifth degrees, nothing may be summoned.

In the one-hundred and twenty-sixth to one-hundred and thirty-second degrees the stars are right for Cthulhu, who appears as a great man with dragon's wings and an octopus' head.

During the one-hundred and thirty-third to one-hundred and thirty-ninth degrees there must be not conjuration.

In the one-hundred and fortieth to one-hundred and forty-sixth degrees the stars are right for Nersel, who appears as an enraged ghoul and is ruler of Zin.

𝕴n the one-hundred and forty-seventh to one-hundred and fifty-third degrees the stars are right of Andryn, who is the weakest of the Old Spirits as he cannot harm the holder of the second ring of Nerexo. If Andryn attacks the magician, he should kiss the ring and speak the word "OROGOT".

𝕴n the one-hundred and fifty-fourth to one-hundred and sixtieth degrees the stars are right for Unspeterus, who appears like a huge black toad.

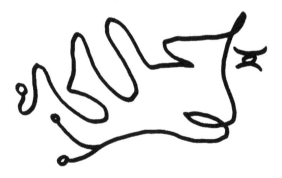

In the one-hundred and sixty-first to one-hundred and sixty-seventh degrees the stars are right for Bas-Juob, who appears like a great slimy maggot with the tentacles of a sea dragon.

In the one-hundred and sixty-eight to one-hundred and sevent-fourth degrees the stars are right for Astursoth, who appears as a great moaning mass, the sounds which echo from it's heart are enough to make men fall and die.

𝕴n the one-hundred and seventy-fifth to one-hundred and eighty-first degrees the stars are right for Azalu, who appears as a great plant beast with many arms and heads.

𝕴n the one-hundred and eighty-second to one-hundred and eighty-eight degrees the stars are right for Leasynoth, who appears like a great dragon and worm, who lived beneath the mountains in the time of the Old Spirits ruling.

In the one-hundred and eighty-ninth to one-hundred and ninety-fifth degrees the stars are right for Yog-Thothai, who appears like a huge, screaming bat with crawling worms for a face. Yog-Thothai can travel far away, sometimes carrying prey to distant stars.

In the one-hundred and ninety-sixth to two-hundred and second degrees the stars are right for Maphleus, who appears as a huge shapeless form which can divide into many smaller forms.

𝕴n the two-hundred and third to two-hundred and ninth degrees, the stars are right for Nun-Hanish and her brood, who appear as a whole army of ghouls, which may travel into men's dreams.

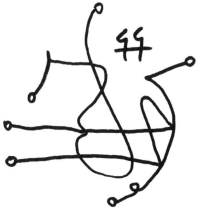

𝕴n the two-hundred and tenth to two-hundred and sixteenth degrees the stars are right for Bas-Lesifa, who appears as a dark orb which cannot be harmed and spreads a plague of madness all around.

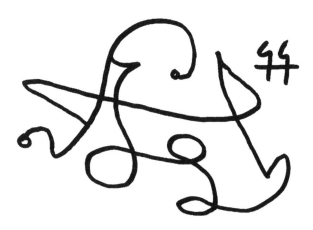

In the two-hundred and seventeenth to two-hundred and twenty-third degrees the stars are right for Meme-myet-Raha and her children, who appear as vast and slimy horned beasts.

During the two-hundred and twenty-fourth to two-hundred and twenty-eighth degrees the stars are most wrong and no evocation may take place.

In the two-hundred and thirty-ninth to two-hundred and forty-fourth degrees the stars are right for Azathoth, who appeareth as a vast and shapeless form of screaming souls and he will be most angry at being drawn away from his secret space.

In the two-hundred and forty-fifth to two-hundred and fifty-first degrees the stars are right for Paturnigish, who appears as a great cloud.

In the two-hundred and fifty-second to two-hundred and fifty-eigth degrees the stars are right for Daga-on, who appears as a gigantic man with the face of a long toothed fish.

In the two-hundred and fifty-ninth to two-hundred and sixty-fifth degrees the stars are right for Ayam, who appears like a great tree made of flesh.

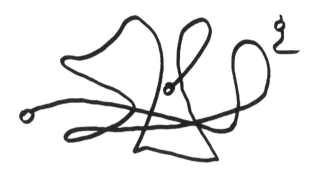

In the two-hundred and sixty-sixth to two-hundred and seventy-second degrees the stars are right for Etananesoe, the true face of Nyarlathotep.

In the two-hundred and seventy-third to two-hundred and seventy-ninth degrees the stars are right for Bugg, who appears like a great furry snake man.

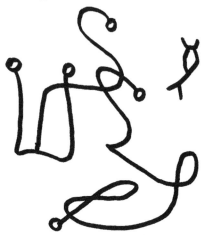

In the two-hundred and eightieth to two-hundred and eighty-sixth degrees the stars are right for Yog-Sothoth, who appears like a great nothingness, a gate which leads outside onto the surface of his vast body.

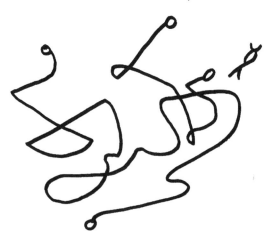

During the two-hundred and eighty-seventh to the two-hundred and ninety-third degrees no conjurations may take place.

In the two-hundred and ninety-fourth to three-hundredth degrees the stars are right for Moivoo, who appears in a form so complex that no man can describe him.

In the three-hundred and first to three-hundred and seventh degrees the stars are right for Beeluge, who appears like a huge lizard with the mouth of an insect.

𝕴n the three-hundred and eighth to three-hundred and fourteenth degrees the stars are right for Caim, who appears like a hissing spider thing.

𝕴n the three-hundredth and fifteenth to three-hundred and twenty-first degrees the stars are right for Lusoath, who appears like a great cone of crystal, which no man should touch, or else his mind be stolen away.

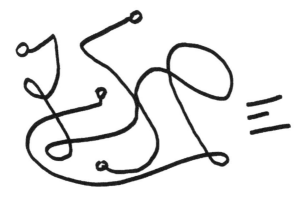

In the three-hundred and twenty-second to three-hundred and twenty-eigth degrees the stars are right for Lusoath, who appears like a great walking mass of earth.

In the three-hundred and twenty-ninth to three-hundred and thirty-fifth degrees the stars are right for Tsapetae, who appears like a great swirling darkness.

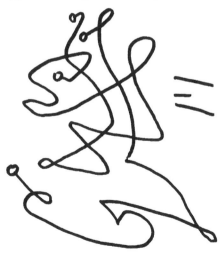

In the three-hundred and thirty-sixth to three-hundred and forty-second degrees the stars are right for Nun-Buhan, who will appear all around the magician like a great horde of worms.

In the three-hundred and forty-third to three-hundred and forty-ninth degrees the stars are right for Hasariel, who will appear like a large flying fiend.

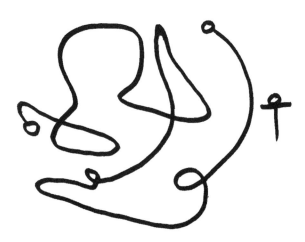

In the three-hundred and fiftieth to three-hundred and fifty-sixth degrees the stars are right for Carr-Vephat, who will appear like a vast mass with dark globes circling all around.

In the three-hundred and fifty-seventh to third degrees the star are right for Detathit, who appears like a river of grabbing hands and dragon's heads.

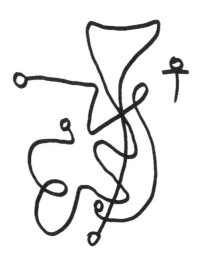

During the fourth to sixth degrees there must be no conjuration and you must carry out the Great Banishing ritual.

Now that you know their times, names and seals I shall once more urge you never to summon any of them except in very exceptional and important situations - if you are a ruler than I tell you neeveer to summon them for battle, or else chaos will ensure. If you are curious I tell you never to summon them to satisfy that curiosity or much terror and death will come of it. If you would manipulate them to bring you your desired then summon them not, but instead conjure a name of Nyarlathotep, for the Old Sprits will not heed your desires because they have no masters. You must also know that there is no way to banish the Old Spirits, they shall only depart when the stars change and become wrong for them.

Liber Tertium

In this book I shall explain the creation of the magical tools that the magician will need to summon the spirits which I have told of in the last two chapters. Take care to construct the tools exactly as I tell you and as I have been told by the names of the hours, for if you do not then they will hold no power. I know of the tools for the lesser conjurations, those of the names of the hours, and I know of the tools which the magician shall use to conjure the Old Spirits - but I only know a few methods of protection against the Old Spirits. For this reason I pray that you will summon the names of Etonetatae, Badero and Nerexo and command them to speak truly to you and to tell you of any protective devices which are available against the Old Spirit which you seek to conjure.

In all matters of conjuration you will need the cardinal tools of the wand, the knife, the perfume, the fire and the parchments. When one would conjure the Old Spirits you will also need the sword, the stones and the ring. Additional to all these things the magician must be wearing the appropriate clothing, which bears the appropriate seals and signs.

*F*irstly the robe is to be made of black material and should be a hooded garment. The robe is to be a new robe made of the magicians hand and should never be used for anything but the work - else it will be spoiled. Starting upon the first day of the week you must do the following - In the hour of Venus you should make the final stitch in the garment and keep it hidden until the next day. On the next day, in the hour of Mercury you should create the following seal on the left arm of the garment and keep it hidden until the next day.

On the next day, in the hour of the Moon you should create the following seal on the right arm of the garment and keep it hidden until the next day.

On the next day, in the hour of Saturn you should create the following seal on the genital area of the garment and keep it hidden until the next day.

On the next day, in the hour of Jupiter you should create the following seal on the back of the garment and
keep it hidden until the next day.

On the next day, in the hour of Mars you should create the following seal on the front of the garment and keep it hidden until the next day. Take care to reproduce it exactly as it appears, for this is the most important of the seals which you will make on the garment.

On the final day, in the hour of the Sun, take the robe from its resting place. Before you continue check it for any imperfections in the patterns and once you are sure of their perfection you may commence with the consecration of the robe. For all of the tools which are concerned with the lesser conjurings, you shall use the following consecration, but for the tools which will only be used to conjure the Old Spirits you shall use a later consecration. The consecration is thus; You shall take boughs of laurel and build a fire, which you shall light as the hour in which you commenced the work is quarter through. Now, before the fire, with the tool in your hands, above the flames, not so low that it shall burn or be damaged and not so high that it will not be touched by the smoke. you shall speak the following:

Samak daram surabel karameka amuranas

Ekotos mirat-fortin ranerug +

Dalerinter marban porafin +

Herikoramonus derogex +

Iratisinger +

I call thee, O mighty names of the hours,

The faces of the faceless Nyarlathotep, +

That you may become one in this hour,

To watch my art be done,

That you will grant this tool which I have fashioned,

The power that it is right to have,

For I have created it in the image of perfection,

And it cannot be undone, +

Iratisinger +

Herikoramonus derogex +

Dalerinter marban porafin +

Ekotos mirat-fortin ranerug +

Samak daram surabel karameka amuranas +

Sedhi! +

Ihdes! +

In the all binding name of Nyarlathotep,

Give power this tool, +

Give power. +

Doros serod! + + +

This conjuration shall be comitted to memory, and shall always be done without book or parchment. Where in this conjuration and where throughout the remainder of the book I write + this shall be the signal for the conjurer to make the sign that gains the attention of the names of the Nyarlathotep and aids them in their coming. This sign is simple and shall be done with the left hand. You should touch your forehead with two of your fingers, then you should draw them down to the chest and touch the heart. Then the fingers should touch the left shoulder, the forehead once more and then the right shoulder.

ow that the robe has been made you shall fashion the wand. In the day following the construction of the robe, in the hour of Venus, you should cut the branch of a cypress tree and carve it into a smooth wand, being just over one foot in length. You should also be wearing your robe during the construction of the tools and you shall keep all of your tools wrapped in the robe, which you shall keep hidden. Having carved the wand on the next day you shall take a knife which is pure and has hurt no-one and in the hour of Mercury shall write these signs on the knife:

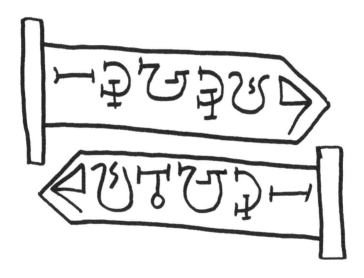

[Note: The triangular sign is a representation of the path of the fingers in the cross sign described above]

Then in that same hour you shall consecrate the dagger and place it in the fire that it shall be cleansed. On the day that follows, in the hour of the Moon, you shall engrave the sign of Ekotos on the wand. The sign should be engraved four times along the length of the wand, the wand should then be turned to the next quarter and the sign engraved four more times. Repeat this until you have come full circle and the wand has sixteen representations of the seal upon it, which is thus:

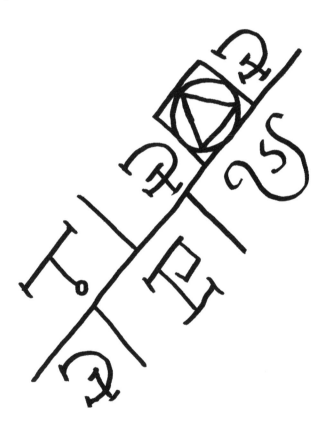

Then, at the top of the wand make the ring of Mirat-Fortin, which is thus:

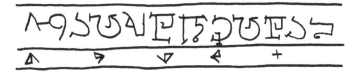

On the day that follows, in the hour of Saturn, you shall consecrate the wand.

Now the perfume should be made and you shall always make it on Monday, in the Moons hour and you shall always consecrate it halfway through the Moons hour on the day in which you have made it. You should take equal parts of mint, frankincense, wormwood, sage, sandalwood, storax and musk, which you will mix together and create a powder from. This powder shall be kept in a bottle which is purple in colour and has the following seal inscribed on its stopper, which shall be made of iron:

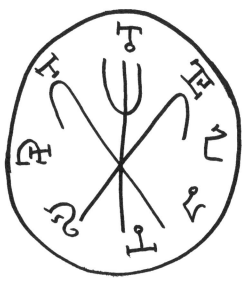

The fire shall be constructed before any act of conjuration takes place and shall be left to burn at the north of the circle for quarter of an hour before the conjuration takes place. It should be made of laurel and cypress wood and once lit, you should say the blessing. If you have not built a circle then one should be made one hour before the conjuration takes place and it can then be left there permenently or erased. For the lesser conjurations a circle made of flour, chalked upon a floor, or cut into the earth will suffice, however, for the greater conjurations, those of the Old Spirits, the circle should be cut into the ground and then filled in with a mixture flour and silver - else the conjurer shall surely die. Having built the circle the conjurer must make the blessing. If he seeks to conjure a name of Nyarlathotep then the conjuration which has been used for the other items shall suffice. If the conjurer seeks to summon the Old Spirits then the Great Consecration should be made, which will follow later in this book.

The final tool which you will require for the lesser conjurations are the parchments, upon which you shall write any conjurations and subjugations which you shall need during the work. The parchments should be written in the day before the work will take place at the hour at which it shall take place on the next day. You shall write upon pure, virgin parchment with ink that has been consecrated for the conjuration in question.

$\mathfrak{J}$f the magician would seek to conjure the Old Spirits, then he shall need several additional tools. The first tool is the sword, which like the dagger shall not have harmed any person or animal. Take this sword in the hour of Mercury and upon the sword engrave the following signs:

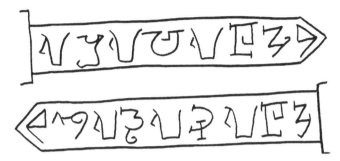

$\mathfrak{T}$he tools which you shall need in conjuring the Old Spirits shall be kept separate from those used in the lesser conjurations and each shall be wrapped in dark green silk, upon which the seal of Unity has been sewn and it is thus:

The sword should be wrapped in this silk and kept hidden. For the space of one moon, each night in the hour of Mercury you shall pray infront of the sword, which you shall keep wrapped in the cover. And you shall pray thus:

+++

Samak daram surabel karameka amuranas

Ekotos mirat-fortin ranerug +

Dalerinter marban porafin +

Herikoramonus derogex +

Iratisinger +

Axarath Malakath +

+++

Axarath Malakath +

Iratisinger +

Herikoramonus derogex +

Dalerinter marban porafin +

Ekotos mirat-fortin ranerug +

Samak daram surabel karameka amuranas +

Sedhi! +

Ihdes! +

+++

This is the prayer of the Great Consecration and you should commit it into memory as with the consecration which has gone before. After the space of one moon has passed you shall take the sword and in the hour of Mercury you shall make a fire. You shall then anoint the sword with the perfume, which has been mixed in part with water. Then you shall hold the sword above the fire at the same hight as before - not so it is in the flames and not so that the smoke cannot touch it. Then you shall pronounce the Great Consecration, which is thus:

Samak daram surabel karameka amuranas

Ekotos mirat-fortin ranerug +

Dalerinter marban porafin +

Herikoramonus derogex +

Iratisinger +

Axarath Malakath +

I call thee, O spirits of the starry band,

I call thee, O Old Spirits,

I call thee from your places or rest

That you may come unto me, +

And watch my art be done, +

In your names I have fashioned this tool,+

And in your names I shall pledge it,+

By your powers I pray that you will grant the tool

The power that it is right to have, +

In the names of

Uk-Han, +

Tursoth, +

Cthuhanai, +

Bovadoit, +

Cthulhu, +

Unspeterus, +

Leasynoth, +

Mememyet-Raha, +

Paturnigish, +

Bugg, +

Beeluge, +

Nun-Buhan,+

I command thee to consecrate this tool,

For I have created it in the image of perfection,

And it cannot be undone, +

Axarath Malakath +

Iratisinger +

Herikoramonus derogex +

Dalerinter marban porafin +

Ekotos mirat-fortin ranerug +

Samak daram surabel karameka amuranas +

Sedhi! +

Ihdes! +

In the all binding name of Mirat-Fortin,

Give power this tool, +

Give power. +

Doros serod! + + +

The Great Consecration shall also be memorised by the magician. Upon finishing the great conescration you shall place the sword into the fire that it may be consecrated in the name of the Old Spirits. When the fire has consumed itself you shall leave the sword to become cold once more and then place it in its cover where it shall remain hidden until it is called for.

Next you shall make the stones, which shall be used to mark the circle when you would conjure the Old

Spirits, for it pleases them. You should take twelve stones
and they shall all be like to the size of your fist and the
stones which you collect shall be Lapis Lazuli, Amber, Onyx,
Bloodstone, Agate, Obsidian, Turquoise, Topaz, Coral, Jet,
Quartz and Jade. You shall keep these stones wrapped in
a similar covering to the sword and shall keep them hidden. You shall also cite the prayer of the Great Consecration for the cycle of one moon as with the sword, but this
shall be done in the hour of the Moon. After the course of
one moon you shall perform the Great Consecration upon
each stone, having first engraved them with the appropriate
signs. Upon the stone of Lapis Lazuli engrave the sign which
I have placed next to the seals for the Spirits who may be
conjured between seven and thirty-fourth degrees. Upon
the stone of Amber engrave the sign which I have placed
next to the seals of the Spirits who may be conjured between
thirty-five and sixty-two degrees. Upon the stone of Onyx
engrave the sign which I have placed next to the seals of the
Spirits who may be conjured between sixty-three and ninety
degrees. Upon the Bloodstone engrave the sign which I have
placed next to the seals of the Spirits who may be conjured
between ninety-one and and one-hundred and twenty-five
degrees. Upon the stone of Agate engrave the sign which I
have placed next to the seals of the Spirits who may be conjured between one-hundred and twenty-six and one-hundred and fifty-three degrees. Upon the stone of Obsidian
engrave the sign which I have placed next to the seals of
the Spirits who may be conjured between one-hundred and
fifty-four and one-hundred and eighty-one degrees. Upon
the stone of Turquoise engrave the sign which I have placed
next to the seals of the Spirits who may be conjured between
one-hundred and eighty-two and two-hundred and sixteen
degrees. Upon the stone of Topaz engrave the sign which I
have placed next to the seals of the Spirits who may be conjured between two-hundred and seventeen and two-hun-

dred and forty-four degrees. Upon the Coral engrave the sign which I have placed next to the seals of the Spirits who may be conjured between two-hundred and forty-five and two-hundred and seventy-two degrees. Upon the stone of Jet engrave the sign which I have placed next to the seals of the Spirits who may be conjured between two-hundred and seventy-three and three-hundred degrees. Upon the stone of Quartz engrave the sign which I have placed next to the seals of the Spirits who may be conjured between three-hundred and one and three-hundred and thirty-five degrees. Upon the stone of Jade engrave the sign which I have placed next to the seals of the Spirits who may be conjured between three-hundred and thirty-six and three degrees. After each stone is consecrated place it upon the cover which the seal of Unity has been made upon. You shall consecrate them in the order which I have written them above and once more keep them hidden until the time of their use is at hand.

The final tool which shall be required is the ring, which shall offer some small protection to the magician who would conjure the Old Spirits, though the protection may be small it would certainly be most foolish to attempt to summon the Old Ones without it. The ring of gold and disc of silver shall be forged in the hour of Saturn and kept hidden, wrapped in green silk upon which the seal of Unity has been made. In the hour of Saturn, on the day that follows the forging of the ring, you shall engrave these characters upon the ring:

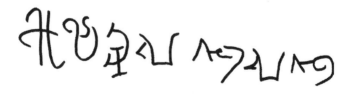

And upon the disc you shall engrave these characters:

Once more, for the space of one moon you shall keep the ring wrapped and pray the prayer of the Great Consecration before it. When the moon has made its cycle you shall perform the Great Consecration in the hour of Saturn, having first anointed the ring with a mixture made from the perfume, flour and water. As with the sword, the ring shall be cast into the fire once the Great Consecration has come to an end. Now that the ring has been created, should you feel the Old Spirits attempt to penetrate the circle you shall kiss the ring and say ABROSAX, for this will strengthen the circle for a small time. But you must remember that there is no permenant protection from them and they will break through the circle in a short time whatever protection you may have.

Liber Quartum

This book will give the magician instruction on how he shall create the circle. As I have said before, the circle should be made strong enough to hold out the spirits for the duration of the conjuration. Should you seek to conjure on of the many faces of Nyarlathotep then the circle may be made from flour, chalk or cut into the earth with the knife or sword. If you would seek to conjure the Greater Spirits then the circle must be cut into the earth or into stone and then it must be filled in with flour and silver dust, for silver offers most excellent protection against the spirits, as does the stone Kinocetus, which may also be powdered for the purpose of strengthening the circle. The form of the circle is thus;

and it shall be made to the size of nine feet and it may be made for permenant of temporary use. At the north of the circle, three feet away, you will place the seal of the spirit which you wish to call. And the seal shall be written upon a circle of one foot of fine lamb skin or parchment. The ink used shall be that of a white pigeons blood, which shall be killed with the knife and the blood collected in a new bowl. A pen shall be made from a feather of the bird. The creation of the circle and the seal shall be done eight hours prior to the rite of conjuration. If you would seek to evoke the Old Spirits then you must make the circle in the hour of Mercury, being eight hours before the conjuration. Once it has been created, the circle should not be entered until the ritual of evocation commences and the seal should be kept wrapped in white silk before the circle. And at the passing of every hour leading up to the ritual you shall banish and wandering spirits from the working area. First you shall make the Sign four times, saying each time: Iratisinger herikoramonus derogex Dalerinter.

Then you shall speak the following:

Away! Away!

I command all wandering spirits to depart in peace

I command you, depart or face my wrath.

I am the he who howls the forgotten names,

I am he who shall bring forth the spirit n.!

Turn and face me, for I hold the Sign!

+ + +

Iratisinger +

Herikoramonus +

Derogex +

Daleringer +

Now depart with haste!

Responsibility Disclaimer

The Author and Publisher take no responsibility on how the contents of this book will be used by the reader and what

Printed in Poland
by Amazon Fulfillment
Poland Sp. z o.o., Wrocław

64638331R00045